CONTENTS

Published by Pedigree Books Limited
The Old Rectory, Matford Lane, Exeter EX2 4PS
E-mail books@pedigreegroup.co.uk
Published in 2002

£5.99

S CLUB 7

RACHEL

Name: Rachel Lauren Stevens

Date Of Birth: 9th April 1978

Starsign: Aries

From: Barnet, North London

Family: Mum Linda, dad Michael, brothers Jason and Leigh. "My parents always told me to do my best - in whatever I was doing, and that's stuck with me."

Previous fashion disasters: "When I was 13 I had a disastrous perm, my hair was just a big mass of curls - it was so awful."

Qualifications: GNVQ Diploma in Business of Fashion from the London School of fashion.

Goes out with: Jeremy Edwards from Holby City. "We were friends for a long time before we got seriously involved. We laugh loads, he's funny and charming."

Likes: Going out with friends.

Thinks: "Sexiness comes from within. It's not about wearing low-cut dresses, it's more to do with the vibe you give off. If you have an inner confidence, people respond."

Shops at: Topshop, Zara and Mango, Selfridges and Matches.

Favourite food: Chinese duck with pancakes, Italian and Indian.

S CLUB 7

JO

Name: Jo O'Meara
Date Of Birth: 29th April 1979
Starsign: Taurus
From: Romford, Essex
Family: Mum Babs, dad Dave, sister Julie and brother Shane
Previous jobs: Working at the Spar checkout. Then at a pet shop. "Even when I was there I didn't mind clearing up the poo. I don't care about things like that - poo is poo innit?"
Previous fashion disasters: When I was 13 I had a disastrous perm.
Gets annoyed by: "Bradley because he's good at winding me up but I will always get my own back."
Goes out with: Long-standing boyfriend Lee. "I was with him a long time before S Club, we've got a special relationship, we believe in what we've got together."
Hangs out with: Rachel, they even shared an apartment at the beginning of filming in Barcelona.
Hates: Her legs "They're too stumpy and short. I would like somebody like Ru Paul's legs - I know he's a man, but women would kill to have legs like that."
Thinks: "I know it's odd but teeth are so sexy. My boyfriend has got **the** teeth. They're just perfect."
Favourite food: Chocolate - chocolate ice cream, chocolate sauce, chocolate bars and chocolate cake etc etc.

S CLUB 7

BRADLEY

Name: Bradley John McIntosh
Date Of Birth: 8th August 1981
Starsign: Leo
From: London
Family: Mum Loraine, dad Steve, step-mom Anne Marie, two sisters I brother.
Previous fashion disasters: He must hide all his bad-hair days under those bandanas.
Hates: Having nothing to do and flat cola.
Likes: Being in the studio.
Thinks: "Space isn't a colour, it just looks black because there's nothing there."
Spend his time: Producing and writing music for other up and coming artists.
Goes on holiday: Hardly ever. "When I get time off I want to hang round with all my mates so I normally stay in London and we go out together. There are so many of us it's difficult to arrange a holiday for all of us at once!"
Ambitions: "I want my own club, my own record company. I'd like to do a film or two. I don't wanna do anything serious, just comedy."
Favourite food: Makes a mean jerk chicken - "I'm a wicked cook and always said that if I couldn't do music I'd be a chef or in the army!?".

S CLUB 7

TINA

Name: Tina Ann Barrett
Date Of Birth: 16th September 1976
Starsign: Virgo
From: London
Family: Mum Cheryl and dad Edward
Previous fashion disasters: "When I cut my hair off, a few years ago. I used to have really long hair, I don't know why I decided to cut it, but I just did. There was a case of miscommunication with my hairdresser."
Best night out: "Any night in Ibiza two summers ago, with my boyfriend at the time."
Party trick: "I can twist my arm all the way round with my hand facing the front. It doesn't look too attractive."
Hates: Rude people.
Likes: Hip Hop and Rock.
Goes out with: "I've got a boyfriend and we've been seeing each other for a while."
Thinks: "Sexiness is all in the twinkley eyes and nice smile I reckon. I don't like clean cut guys. I prefer a bit of a rough edge."
Reads: Cosmopolitan and In Style.
Could not live without: Television, "I love Graham Norton and Frasier."

S CLUB 7

JON

Name: Jon Lee

Date Of Birth: 26th April 1982

Starsign: Taurus

From: Devon, South England

Family: Mum Wendy, dad Terry, brothers Jamie and Ben and sister Cassie.

Music qualification: Grade five piano.

Previous jobs: Has been working in the theatre since he was 12, including lead in the musical Oliver! Went to stage school.

Goes out with: No one at the moment, but then he might be lying... "For years, when I was asked if I had a girlfriend, I told people I was single even if I did have a girlfriend at the time."

Hates: The paparazzi hanging around everywhere S Club go out.

Likes: His dog Molly, but he's stopped going on about her. "I was starting to sound like this obsessed nutter who was having a love affair with his dog, which wasn't the case at all."

Spends his time: Horse riding - he's just bought a horse called Polly.

Thinks: Every now and again!

Reads: Has been meaning to get into the Harry Potter books.

HANNAH

Name: Hannah Louise Spearritt
Date Of Birth: 1st April 1981
Starsign: Aries
From: Great Yarmouth
Family: Mum Jenny, dad Michael, older sister Tanya, and older brother Stuart
Goes out with: Paul Cattermole
Looks like: Emma Bunton? "People do say I look like her, but everywhere I go I get told I look like someone else. I've been described as Geri Halliwell, Cameron Diaz and Goldie Hawn."
Spends her time: Chillin' at home, watching films and trashy TV, playing pool and trying to cook!
Hates: Not being able to get a curry in Barcelona.
Likes: Long drives and camping.
Thinks: Life is absolutely fabulous!
Favourite food: Japanese, bangers and mash.

CLUB 7

PAUL

Name: Paul Cattermole
Date Of Birth: 7th March 1977
Starsign: Pisces
From: St Albans
Family: Mum Liz, sister Treena and two brothers Colin and Martin.
Went to: The National Youth Music Theatre and met Hannah during a production of Pendragon. "We performed together in Hong Kong and on Broadway in New York. It's was wicked."
Previous jobs: "I had two paper rounds - with two rival newsagents. I had to deliver about 200 newspapers a morning and got £50 a week." Plus theatre doorman and ceramic hygienist.
Goes out with: Hannah, their close friendship grew into something more romantic....
Worst habit: "Chewing my nails.
Likes: His Playstation.
Wears in bed: Boxers.
Favourite food: Burgers and chips.

Wordsearch 1

Can you find all the words below hidden in the grid mix?

Y	E	T	T	T	H	H	A	N	N	A	H	S	S	I	D
B	O	O	G	W	R	B	Y	O	U	O	O	X	S	E	O
B	L	U	C	O	O	R	R	U	M	I	T	A	U	E	N
O	R	M	R	O	B	I	U	A	G	F	Y	U	N	D	T
T	H	I	G	E	G	G	N	M	D	T	D	T	O	I	S
C	H	I	N	L	M	G	P	A	U	L	H	P	R	N	T
C	E	G	I	G	E	Y	L	S	M	Y	E	G	T	A	O
A	L	N	I	T	I	R	N	A	P	I	L	Y	I	R	P
R	R	S	O	N	G	T	U	U	B	U	L	C	S	R	M
N	O	J	E	L	I	M	A	I	M	G	U	L	G	N	O
I	T	D	S	S	I	A	N	L	H	B	R	I	I	O	V
V	R	A	C	H	E	L	D	Y	L	E	E	A	T	O	I
A	M	N	E	G	N	I	S	I	A	B	M	R	U	L	N
L	O	C	F	U	N	A	S	C	R	I	A	K	O	K	G
A	V	E	J	A	A	P	H	U	M	F	T	C	E	N	X
L	E	V	O	L	D	N	A	E	C	A	E	P	K	A	E

You
S Club
Reach
Hannah
Paul
Bradley
Bring it all back
Carnival
Fun
Boogie
You're my number one
Peace and love
Jon
Laughs
Don't stop moving
Party
Song
Dance
Tina
Miami
Right guy
Sun
Hot
Rachel

Answers pages 62-63

S CLUB 7

How much do you know about S Club 7? This quiz ranges from easy questions to very difficult, so fill in the quiz and swap results with your pals to see who's the biggest S Club 7 Swot....

1. Whose mum is called Babs?

    _____

2. What was the crocodile called in Miami 7?

    _____

3. Name the S Clubber whose mum sang with the band Bomb the Bass?

    _____

4. Which three TV Talent boys sang with S Club 7 on the Dublin date of their Carnival tour?

    _____

5. Which S Clubbers met at the National Youth Music Theatre

    _____

6. Whose favourite meal is Steak Diane?

    _____

7. Name Tina's first crush.

    _____

CAR TROUBLE?

Who owns which car?

a) Mercedes SLK

b) Peugeot 106

c) Vauxhall Corsa

d) Black Lotus

Answers pages 62-63

SWOT ➡

8. Whose favourite colour is violet?

_____

9. Whose favourite crisps are Walkers cheese and onion?

_____

10. Whose best joke: "What's a flip flop without the flip? A flop flop."

_____

11. Who had a pet mouse during the filming of Hollywood 7?

_____

12. Someone nicks pillows wherever he goes. Who is it?

_____

13. What does Paul have under his bed? A remote control car or a Action Man castle?

_____

14. Who did washing up as a past job?

_____

CARNIVAL TOUR 2002

On the 30th January this year S Club 7 performed their biggest and by far their best tour performing in nine cities across the land, to over 200,000 people. And what a show it was. Over 100 people were involved in creating the show - from the musicians, dancers and make-up artists to the crew who built the enormous set, the truck drivers and the caterers. That's a lot of people, but one thing that came out of the tour was that over the 23 dates everyone really grew to feel that they were part of the S Club 7 family. Aw. The show itself lasted two hours, there were five costume changes per band member and everyone said it was the most gruelling but most satisfying experience yet... let's see how they did it.

With only a fortnight left before the first night in Dublin, we caught up with S Club 7 rehearsing their dance moves in a London studio. They are all a little nervous that they won't quite make it, as the choreography is the most demanding yet and there's a lot to learn in only a short space of time. Paul is finding it a struggle.

"When it comes down to performance day," he says, looking very peaky, "We're up against the wall a bit."

Jon is also admitting things aren't quite done and dusted.

"I think we'll get through it," he says. "I hope we don't pass out half way through or something... So far everyone seems still alive..."

Bradley thinks everyone should focus, Hannah looks like she's struggling with some of the dance moves, but Jo and Tina are getting into the swing of things. Tina, being an ex-dancer, finds it easier: "It's been drilled in me to pick up routines." Rachel finds it tough, "but it's good," she says. "We're getting a lot of exercise and building up our stamina."

This tour is the Carnival Tour 2002 and Priscilla Samuels, tour producer and choreographer, describes the feel of the show: "Some of the music has been changed to be more carnival-like, more Latin-influenced and Samba-influenced," she says. The dance moves reflect that and she can see that her rigorous instruction is a big deal for the sultry samba-movin' S Club 7. "That's the biggest challenge for them," she says. "Keeping up the pace. The best piece of advice I could give them would be feel like every show is your first and your last."

Priscilla has one thing on her mind: perfection. She's worked with the band for years so they know her well and trust her completely. Priscilla gets results. Bradley thinks the world of her.

"She's the only person I want to be like," he says, frothing with praise. "Focus-wise and performing-wise; she's taught us a lot of stuff along the way. She's made us believe in ourselves."

Ooh, but she's tough.

When the band go and see the set, they are stunned. It's absolutely enormous, very high-tech and glitzy. "The stage is very *'Come on down'*," says Hannah, " I like it a lot." Jon thinks it looks like a disco, which was probably what Hannah meant too.

The stage takes approximately six hours to put up, and three hours to dismantle. This has to happen every time S Club 7

change venues, which is why there's so many sturdy roadie types on the tour. Along with a huge video screen behind the band and a catwalk which is built *over* the audience for one section of the show, there's a big trap door effect which will be used throughout the show. Seven lifts raise each band member from under the stage to right on it - they literally "pop up" - and the group's first task is to practise standing very still on their individual platform as they ping up and down. Jo is wary at first but she and the others find it a bit of a wheeze and can't stop whizzing up and down once they've started. Come on you lot, there's still work to do.

Seyara Sami teaches the group vocal warm-up techniques before the tour, "so they don't go out there screaming," she says. "I'm making sure they're blending their voices together in the right way - singing lead in a solo part is different to singing in a group," she finishes.

CARNIVAL TOUR 2002

Priscilla is watching them intensely, directing all the moves. They know she won't accept anything less than amazing.

Hannah still thinks there's lots to do and Bradley agrees. "It's blending the singing and the dancing, putting it together," he says. "I confuse myself, if I think about my harmonies I forget the dance routine, and if I think about dancing I forget the singing."

The group have to rehearse one song about twenty times, so they can remember the words and harmonies. Then they have to remember the dance routines on top of that; no wonder they all look a bit worried still.

There are seven dancers - three girls and four boys. They're just as excited - and nervous - as the band. "It's my first tour," says Peter Francis. "I've never worked in a big group situation." Their job is to fill the stage throughout the show with colour and dance, mirroring and complementing S Club 7 moves. Even they - professional dancers - are finding it a challenge, "We're getting really fit!" says Kate Eloise. "It's a *real* challenge."

Gayla Aspinall who works for 19 Management Entertainment and is the tour director, is dedicated to making the show the best ever. "The first week has been pretty full-on," she says. "But the band love touring and being up on stage, they get on with it and put in their best efforts." She's not only concerned with the band, she oversees everything. A few days before the first show the lighting and the video wall are not right and Gayla has to make sure they are. The hydraulic lifts are the most complicated part of the show as there are 60 computer-controlled winches needed to control them, therefore it requires a lot of practise, moving them up and down. The band, now rehearsing on the stage set-up in London, have still not got it licked. There's a disco section in the show which everyone is really excited about, but this is the section that really stretches them. "It's very hard," says Jon. 'We haven't got it down to a tee yet."

The last day of rehearsals is known as the day of reckoning. Kenny Ho the costume designer is checking all the costumes. "Everything's got to be pukka and it will be," he says, sewing needle in hand. "The big-wigs are coming down to see it." By this he means the head of S Club 7 management and record company. Gayla also knows they have to impress. "People haven't seen it yet, this is the final run through, and if it's not good now…" she trails off, obviously preoccupied with the show. Priscilla is charging around making last minute changes. All Jon can say is that he's deciding whether or not to be sick. Oh dear.

Nicki Chapman, from 19 Entertainment, is looking forward to it. "This is their second tour, but you still get nervous for them," she says.

As the band go through the show and really give it their all, the assembled crowd look like their really enjoying it. The band themselves look like they're really having the time of their lives - everything seems to have come together and Jon has not been sick!

Priscilla is ecstatic at the end of the run-through. "Its' excellent, the best rehearsal they've done," she says, grinning from ear to ear.

Hannah notices that everyone is smiling. "I can't wait to do it now," say Jon. It's the final day of rehearsals and S Club 7 are in Dublin at Point Depot. This afternoon there are two run-throughs in full costume for everyone. Jon, as optimistic as ever, thinks they'll forget everything.

Paul has started this tour with a radical change of image, he's dyed his hair blonde and it's very, very short. Jon says "he just wants to be a bit more like me," but he's kidding. Probably.

"I like it," says Paul. "It's good for the tour, it's just... good full stop."

After the wonderful rehearsal last week there have been last minute changes, *You're My Number One* has been added and with a new routine for everyone to learn.

"When we watched the show as a whole" says Gayla, "It was obvious that we had too many songs next to each other all at mid or low tempo. So we need to add in one fans would know into the show."

Priscilla is not happy, she thinks the last run-through was nowhere near as good as Thursdays. She's says what she thinks to the band, "I show no sympathy in that way," she barks. "They've got to get on with it". Yikes. But Jon agrees, they've got to polish their show.

"She needs to see it as it's going to be," he says. "She needs to know we're ready to stand in front of 10,000 people and do it."

The excitement about tonight's performance has also turned into... silliness. He and Jo act the goon.

The nerves are really starting to show. Rachel says her nerves have come early. With a few hours to go before the show. She can't eat anything and sits looking... well, nervous. "They're good nerves, though," she says.

The fans are all queuing up outside and the atmosphere *in* the venue is one of intense excitement with kids and their parents leaping around to support act S Club Juniors, who are going down a treat.

Backstage, nerves are getting worse. Hannah claims her arms "feel weird". Hm. Bradley plays Playstation and looks calm. He says he likes to "hype up, but first of all I like to chill out and savour my energy for later on." Paul is similarly cool, so now he's worried about that.

The show starts and audience are quiet… mostly. The lights go up on the stage and we see the dancers thumping a rhythm on the drums. Then S Club 7 emerge from their trap doors and the place erupts - it's difficult at first to hear the start of *S Club Party* the cheers are so loud. Paul, Hannah, Rachel, Tina, Jon, Jo and Bradley give it their all and it looks spectacular.

The show consists of different sections, the band's favourite being the "Disco" section where they sing *Dance Dance Dance* which is a real winner. Bradley stands behind a DJ Booth and the band dance and sing around. Jon is very proud of his solo song, *Long and Winding Road* which he sings at the piano. Bradley gets to perform the smooth *Right Guy* with Paul and Jon all dressed in shiny suits and trilby hats, very sharp, lads. Jo is especially proud of her ballad section, which gives her a chance to show off her lung power, especially on *Never Had A Dream Come True*. The show ends with the band on the catwalk, which is raised above the crowd, and the last songs of the set are *Reach* then a reprise of *Bob Marley, Michael Jackson and Arrow*, which has the band getting the whole crowd on their feet (including the mums and dads) and dancing along. S Club 7 give it so much welly you might mistake them for farmers. What a bunch of pros. Afterwards, the band are thrilled, they've pulled it off big time. Everyone gathers backstage to congratulate the group.

In the Mix!

Help the band unscramble the words on these discs so they can release their next single.

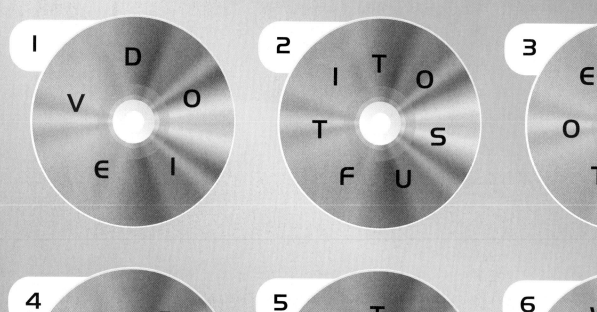

1. D V O E I
2. I T O T S F U
3. E I R O U T N
4. T S O H V W
5. T U O R
6. W N G E O N S

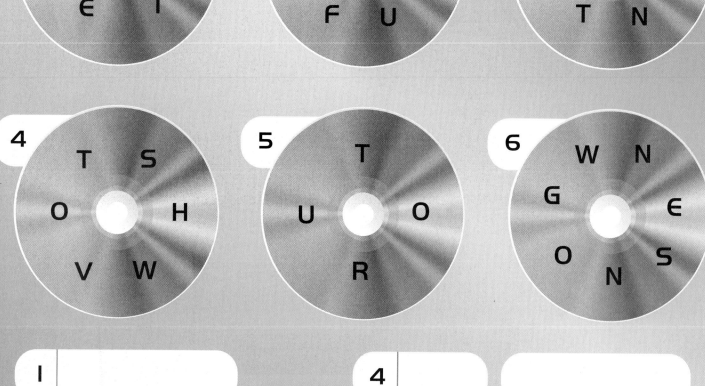

1		4	
2		5	
3		6	

Answers pages 62-63

S CLUB 7 IN QUOTES

Everyone's said silly little things from time to time. and so have S Club 7 - but can you guess who said what?

a) "The last book I read was an astrology book. I was reading all about what Leos are like."

b) "I think men were a bit scared of me even when I was single - they certainly aren't going to start now."

c) "I'd like to go to the moon and eat cheese. Did you know its made of Wensleydale and Saturn is made of Brie?"

d) "I'd love to have my own little boutique and clothes line."

e) "Space is purple."

f) "I can bite my toenails."

g) "When I'm thinking about something serious my nose twitches."

h) "I think I'm normal but my family might have other ideas."

S CLUB 7 IN QUOTES

i) "Big ones, little ones, spiders just really freak me out."

j) "People expect aliens to be little green men but how do we know what they're like?"

k) "I've never said anything controversial."

l) "Tina's got lovely lips. But not that I want any rumours starting about me."

m) "I love blue Extra chewing gum and always have to have some in my bag."

n) "I would pose in my boxer shorts for a million pounds but that's as far as I'd go."

o) "I do flirt quite a lot and chat people up and I grab people sometimes in a touchy-feely sort of way."

Answers pages 62-63

Where's my Handbag?

Can you help the girls through the maze to find their handbags.

LYRICS

Here are the lyrics to the last three S Club 7 songs for you to sing along to!

CLUB 7

Don't Stop Movin'

Don't stop moving to the funky funky beat
Don't stop moving to the funky funky beat
Don't stop moving to the funky funky beat
Don't stop moving to the S Club beat
DJ got the party started, there's no end in sight
Everybody's movin to the rhythm that's inside
Its a crazy world but tonight's the right situation
Don't get left behind
I can feel the music flowing through me everywhere
Ain't no destination, baby, we don't even care
There's a place to be if you need the right education
Let it take you there
And just go with the magic, baby
I can see it's there in your eyes
Let it flow, stop the waiting
Right here on the dance floor is where you gotta let it go
Don't stop moving
Can you feel the music
DJ's got us going around, 'round
Don't stop moving
Find your own way to it
Listen to the music
Taking you to places that you've never been before baby now
You can touch the moment, almost feel it the air
Don't know where we're going, baby, we don't even care
Ain't no mystery just use your imagination
Let it take you there
And just go with the magic, baby
I can see it there in your eyes
Let it flow, stop the waiting
Right here on the dance floor is where you gotta let it go
Don't stop moving
Can you feel the music
DJ's got us going around, 'round
Don't stop moving
Find your own way to it
Listen to the music
Taking you to places that you've never been before, baby, now

Don't stop moving to the funky funky beat
Don't stop moving to the funky funky beat
Don't stop moving to the funky funky beat
Don't stop moving to the S Club beat
Forget about your fears tonight
Listen to your heart, let's just touch the sky
No need to reason why
Just listen to the sound let it make you come alive
Don't stop moving
Can you feel the music
DJ's got us going around, 'round
Don't stop moving
Find your own way to it
Listen to the music
Don't stop moving
Can you feel the music
DJ's got us going around, 'round
Don't stop moving
Find your own way to it
Listen to the music, taking you to places that you've never
been before, baby, now
Don't stop moving to the funky funky beat
Don't stop moving to the funky funky beat
Don't stop moving to the funky funky beat
Don't stop moving to the S Club beat

Written by: S. Ellis, S. Solomon, S Club7. Published by 19
Music/BMG Music Publishing Ltd., Rondor Music (London)
Ltd, Universal Music Publishing.

YOU

You, you, you, you
You are all I need to get me through (get me through now, baby)
Like a fallin' star I fell for you (fell for you)
Sweet anticipation
It's giving me the butterflies
And my heartbeat's racin'
Cos lovin' you's so beautiful
When you're so irresistible
So don't stop (don't stop)
What you're doin', baby
So good (so good)
And it drives me crazy
One touch, I'm in heaven, yeah
Cos lovin' you's so beautiful, baby
Cos you are all I need to get me through (get me through now, baby)
Like a fallin' star I fell for you (fell for you, yeah)
You taught me how to love
An angel sent from high above
Now I know that all I need is you
Yes, I need you and you need me
And we'll always be together
You're my inspiration
My world just seems a brighter place
I just wanna tell you
I've never ever felt this way
I've never thought I'd see the day
Real love (real love) has come my way
And I know (I know) that it's here to stay
And it feels like never before
Cos lovin' you's so beautiful, baby
Cos you are all I need to get me through (get me through now, baby)

Like a fallin' star I fell for you (fell for you, yeah)
You taught me how to love
An angel sent from high above
Now I know that all I need is you
Yes, I need you and you need me
And we'll always be together
Yes, I need you and you need me
And we'll always be together
You're my inspiration
My world just seems a brighter place
I just wanna tell you
I've never ever felt this way
I've never thought I'd see the day
Real love (real love) has come my way
And I know (I know) that it's here to stay
And it feels like never before
Cos lovin' you's so beautiful, baby
Cos you are all I need to get me through (get me through now, baby)
Like a fallin' star I fell for you (fell for you, yeah)
You taught me how to love
An angel sent from high above
Now I know that all I need is you
You are all I need to get me through (get me through now, baby)
Like a fallin' star I fell for you (fell for you, yeah)
You taught me how to love
An angel sent from high above
Now I know that all I need is you
Yes I need you, and you need me
I need you (oh yeah)
I need you (oh yeah)
I need you (oh yeah)

Written by: E. Kennedy, T. Lever, M. Percy,
T. Woodcock, Published by Sony Music Publishing,
19 Music, BMG Music Publishing Ltd., Steelworks
Songs/Universal Music Publishing.

Have You Ever

Sometimes it's wrong to walk away
Although you think it's over
Knowing there's so much more to say
Suddenly the moments gone
And all your dreams are upside down
And you just wanna change the way the world goes round
Tell me have you ever loved and lost somebody?
Wished there was a chance to say I'm sorry,
Can't you see?
That's the way I feel about you and me, baby.
Have you ever felt your heart was breaking?
Looking down the road you should be taking
I should know
Cos I loved and lost the day I let you go
I can't help but think that this is wrong
We should be together back in your arms where I belong,
Now I've finally realised
It was forever that I found
I'd give it all to change the way the world goes round
Tell me have you ever loved and lost somebody?
Wished there was a chance to say I'm sorry
Can't you see?
That's the way I feel about you and me, baby
Have you ever felt your heart was breaking?
Looking down the road you should be taking
I should know
Cos I loved and lost the day I let you go
I really wanna hear you say
That you know just how it feels
To have it all and let it slip away
Can't you see?
Although the moments gone
After holding on somehow
Wishing I could change the way the world goes round
Tell me have you ever loved and lost somebody?
Wished there was a chance to say I'm sorry
Can't you see?
That's the way I feel about you and me, baby
Have you ever felt your heart was breaking?
Looking down the road you should be taking
I should know
Cause I loved and lost the day I let
Yes I loved and lost the day I let
Yes I loved and lost the day I let you go

Written by: C. Dennis, A. Frampton, C.Braide.
Published by EMI Music Publishing Ltd., Warner
Chappell Music Ltd.

Where am I?

Can you work out where the different members of S Club 7 are standing?
It could be anywhere in the UK and Ireland...

TINA: "I'm standing in the dock, looking at the ferry cross the Mersey, just before I go to Penny Lane."

RACHEL: "I'm eating an oatcake on Princes Street, watching men in kilts."

JON: "I'm in the middle of England standing beside the NEC arena where we often play, having some black pudding."

JO: "I'm sitting on a boat on the Liffey, looking at the students drink their Guinness and I'm sure I can spot someone from Westlife over there..."

HANNAH: "I'm by the seaside on the pier enjoying an ice-cream before I go to the Pavilion."

EDINBURGH

PAUL: "I'm on the Mall looking at the fabulous Changing Of The Guard before I go and get on a bright red bus."

LIVERPOOL

DUBLIN

BIRMINGHAM

CARDIFF

LONDON

BRIGHTON

BRADLEY: "I'm in the Millennium stadium listening to Tom Jones."

33 S CLUB

S CLUB 7

Here's the S Clubbers' favourite snaps that were taken when they filmed their

The S Club 7 crew standing in a line, by some boats. Nice weather!

Hannah and Paul have a quick natter.

Don't fall off that ledge, Paul!

Jon looking hot!

Bradley looking... awake!

Rachel looking cool

SNAPS

third series, Hollywood 7 in Los Angeles...

Jo's cheesey grin

Jo tells Jon a joke...
but was it that funny?

Hannah's seen a mouse!

Or was it all these seven
creatures? Very frightening!

Or was it just Tina and Rachel?

Tina offers a cup of water to the
airplane in case it's thirsty...

CARNIVAL TOUR 2002

PART 2

S Club 7 study their press: the first night of the tour has got lots of reviews and Hannah is slightly bemused by a story that talks about her wearing fishnets on stage, when she only wore them in the last video. Jo gets annoyed because one paper calls the girls "pop babes" and doesn't mention the fantabulous concert very much. Or the boys.

"They only say that," she scolds, "'Cos we've got a bit of belly showing. Obviously they didn't have anything else to write about."

After all the wonderment of the first night, Priscilla is not happy. She loves all of the show apart from the last bit, which she thinks should be "more dramatic, that's why I'm doing little things to change it".

Gayla agrees, "The first night has shown up some problems," she says. The final song is going to be given more choreography, it so it has more impact. "We're all highly critical," continues Gayla. "We want people to come and be thoroughly entertained the whole way through."

S Club learn the moves and the second night has that dynamism, that extra *oomph*.

In the hotel, Jo's worrying about her hair. Her hairdresser cut it because it was breaking off, and Jo hated it. "My mum always tells me, 'Don't get your hair cut 'cos you'll look like a boy!' and my boyfriend was unsure at first and told me I looked like my mum."

Jo hates being away from her boyfriend Lee.

"Sometimes I think it's easier for me when I've gone away, because I'm busy all the time," she says. "I have things to occupy my mind whereas it's harder on him, if he has a day off he sits indoors, bored."

Jo and Rachel have become very close since meeting each other in the band.

"We've got an understanding," smiles Jo. "We're a bit too much like sisters sometimes, we have a lot of arguments but nothing too drastic,.

S CLUB 7

Jo's mum Babs ("the most important person in the world") is here at the Docklands show. She's here with her sister Valda, who looks exactly the same. They are currazy ladies, and sing the oldie *Wooden Heart* into a couple of bananas. Jo looks embarrassed, and gets them to be quiet and talk about the show instead.

"S Club 7 were brilliant tonight," says Babs. "Every kid was standing up, they know all the moves, it's lovely."

When the band get to Manchester they have *more* rehearsals because Priscilla hasn't had enough.

The band go to a local dance studio and tighten up their routines.

"They won't call themselves dancers but everyone's a dancer in their heart of hearts," says Priscilla, smiling.

The dancing is not the only problem. Gayla is grim about technicalities: "Today has been absolute hell," she says. "We've just loaded the set up here, but the venue is the biggest so far and the walkway is a lot higher and more unstable. We have to see how much more it moves when the band dance on it."

The band are slightly worried about getting on the catwalk, thinking it will sway and not wanting to lose their legs. Yes, the stage is too bouncy, but they resolve the technical problem with, er, some technical things.

CARNIVAL TOUR 2002

PART 2

The show tonight is even better than before, and the band are really getting comfortable with it all. But - uh-oh - Priscilla's still got a few words to say. "I think there was a little fire on stage on *Never Had Dream Come True*," she says. "There was too much smoke, I couldn't see anyone."

By the middle of the tour everyone's settled into it and they're confident before the performance each night. As we roll on to London, Bradley is very keen to do his best.

"I want the same vibe as when I go to a show and it blows you away," he says. "It should be neat, tidy and no slack. Bradley still encourages the crowd to get up and dance along.

When you're singing and dancing two hours every night you have to have one thing: energy.

"Great food is the bonus of touring," says Bradley, who likes to tuck into a hot meal before the show. "You need to eat or you'll faint on stage," says Priscilla. Jo's speciality pudding for maximum energy is ice cream and chocolate sauce. The dressing room they're in has all the essentials: TV, DVD, videos, crisps, fruit, water, soft drinks and scented candles... and also a sofa for Bradley to sleep on. Ah, does Bradley like his kip... he's always found sleeping when there's a lull in the day, when he's having his hair braided, when he spots a sofa/chair/floor.

"It's not easy to be on the ball," says Bradley. "Sometimes I'm chilled and sometimes you won't be able to shut me up. I try my best to hide my feelings,

you won't know whether I'm up or down. I'm always polite, I do want to have conversations, I'm human like everyone else. I have good days and bad days."

The band like performing in London but find it's always more pressured, because their family and friends all come down to watch the show and party afterwards.

Bradley knows that everyone has a stage persona. "When Hannah goes on stage, she comes across as really sexy, giving it large - backstage she's just Hannah, with a cup of tea and biscuit in her hand. Rachel's the same, when she goes out, she's *giving it*. Jo now, she is just a rock chick, banging her head. On stage I feel I'm different.

"Touring is very much about the family you take on the road," he continues. "It's cool when you've got a bigger crew with you, musicians, dancers... after work we all hang out and have a laugh. We know each other well enough to have a good relationship."

The band love being on the road, and some think they should go on longer than five weeks, the length of this tour. Says Jon, "We're doing what we want to do all the time, we don't get a chance to do it that often - only 2% of our job is performing live." Their days are long as they spend their time before their show promoting the single *You* - doing TV, press and record signings.

CARNIVAL TOUR 2002 PART 2

Bradley also loves songwriting and perfecting his singing.

"Writing pop music is hard for me, I start writing a pop tune but by the end it sounds like Busta Rhymes. I have so much more to learn, I just want to write with as many people as I can, musicians and songwriters, just to get little bit of knowledge from everyone. I can sing in tune but nowhere near where I want to be, even with my dancing, I want to be tight." Well, he's not doing too badly, is he?

By the time we get to the last night of the whole tour at Birmingham NEC, everyone is getting teary.

"It is a sad occasion" says Jon. "We've been doing this every day for a long time. Priscilla agrees: "Each person has been saying how much they've been enjoying the show." Everyone has made friends, and some people won't see each other for months - dancers, musicians, the band, the crew. Big blubs all round.

Gayla is made of sterner stuff. "The show is almost over and I have a sense of relief that it's happened, the walkway never fell down…" She says, not blubbing. "It was a successful tour and I'm sad that the show is never to be seen again live."

For the final time the band are driven to the venue to do the soundcheck and they're finding it hard to take the preparations seriously. Tina and Jon are larking around as usual. As they warm up their voices, Jo does pretend opera-type singing, which sounds awful. What larks indeed.

"I don't know how they've done it all," says dancer Cordelia. "They sing live every night, it's amazing."

"You can't take it for granted," says Bradley. "It might not be there tomorrow, we love it."

Priscilla goes through everyone in turn. "Jo goes out on stage like a rock 'n' roll queen, she's so into it. Jon has really progressed vocally, he's a good performer. Rachel is enjoying it, she's challenged by it and pushes herself to the limits. Tina is an ex-dancer, she sees the other dancers behind her and she works harder.

"Paul is having a great time out there," she continues. "I do push him, he's hopefully learnt that he can stay fit, be on stage and do what everyone else does - he's come a long way. Bradley really feels the music."

On the last night, the crew always play pranks on the band.

"Last tour we had a gorilla come on when Rachel was singing," says Gayla. "This time we've got a suitcase at the foot of Jon's piano, which he can't see. Priscilla's assistant Paula comes on in a flat cap and trench coat and wheels the suitcase while he's singing."

CARNIVAL TOUR 2002

PART 2

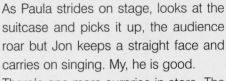

As Paula strides on stage, looks at the suitcase and picks it up, the audience roar but Jon keeps a straight face and carries on singing. My, he is good.

There's one more surprise in store. The whole production team come on stage during the disco section in wigs and big coats and dance along with S Club 7 and the dancers and musicians. They're all having a hoot - letting their hair down after all the stresses and strains of the tour: keeping band, crew and the crowd happy while making sure the stage is working, everything's safe and on time.

After the show, Jon sums up the feeling of being on stage.

"It's amazing, because nearly all the people in the audience would love to trade places with you."

"The parents enjoy it as well," says Jo. "They sometimes get into it more than kids, everyone leaves having had a good time."

Wiping away the tears from their eyes, they are exhausted but still energised by the whole tour. "We'll be back!" they shout. And next year they plan to do something even better and more spectacular.

Let's leave the last word to Priscilla. "They went out to show how much they've grown up since the last tour," she says, proud as punch. "They've achieved so much and they've worked hard for it."

Sofa Search

Help the boys find a comfy couch to kip on...

TRUE OR FALSE

TRUE   **FALSE**

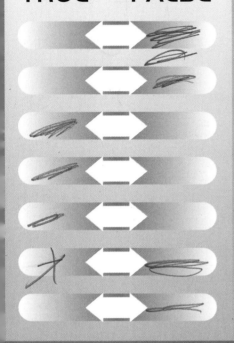

1. Bradley's middle name is 'Excelsior'.

2. Rachel's favourite food is curry.

3. Hannah eats four bananas a day

4. Paul's nickname is 'Gwaks'.

5. Rachel was discovered in Sony Music reception

6. Tina used to be a Vet

7. Jo's mum is called Sandy.

NAME GAME

W¹ e² m³ b⁴ l⁵ e² y⁶

A⁷ r⁸ e² n⁹ d⁷

Using the grid above, fill in the FIRST letter of each ANSWER with the corresponding number to make a S Club 7 Party Venue.

1. Drink a lot of this to stay healthy.
2. You need food to give you this - it helps you jump around.
3. What you play on the CD player, or you hear on the radio.
4. Mr McIntosh's first name.
5. They're not arms, they help you walk.
6. The colour of bananas.
7. Someone who plays a role.
8. The colour of the STOP traffic light.
9. Something that's not old.

Answers pages 62-63

45 S CLUB

S CLUB 7 – WHAT A YEAR!

Not only did S Club 7 win a 2002 BRIT award (their second) for Best Single for Don't Stop Movin', they scooped the ITV Record Of The Year prize for Don't Stop Movin', filmed their 4th TV series and played at the Queen's Golden Jubilee concert...!

They celebrated getting to number 1 with Don't Stop Movin' in April last year handed over £200,000 to Children in Need, which they raised with their charity single Never Had A Dream Come True in 2000 and in 2001 they released Have You Ever for Children in Need, raising another £200,000.

Bradley spoke of his excitement about doing lead vocals on a number one song. "It's the first time I've taken the lead," he said, "And was a bit nervous at first, about how people would react to it.
"I feel really supported by our fans as it went to number 1," he continued. "It's a great song, we love it."

Everyone, it seemed, loved the song and in December 2001 it was made Record Of The Year by the ITV programme. S Club 7 were ecstatic, this was the start of some great achievements.

At the Brits awards in 2002, and up against such people as Blue and Kylie, they won best single and were thrilled. Their first BRIT award for Best British Newcomer would have a friend to stand next to...
Then -then!!! - they were invited to perform in front of the Royals and a host of guests at Buckingham Palace. Not bad, eh? Paul was thrilled to end his time with S Club at such a glittering event, which included the likes of legends Queen and Sir Paul McCartney. The seven also sang with Sir Cliff Richard on a special version of *Move It.* Blimey.

"I couldn't have asked for a better way to go out," said Paul, following the Party in the Palace. When he announced he was quitting earlier in the year he had no idea the Jubilee concert would be his last. "When I realised I couldn't have planned it any better.

"People have been asking me how it feels to be leaving tonight but it hasn't really sunk in yet - the occasion has swamped out any feelings I had, " he continued. "There's a feeling of nostalgia because of all the good laughs we've had, but I'm over the moon to be doing what I'm going to be doing."

AND THEN THERE WERE SIX...

PAUL LEAVES S CLUB 7

It was a difficult decision to make, but after months of thinking hard Paul decided to leave S Club 7 in June this year, after he had fulfilled the band's commitments and been part of the massive Carnival 2002 tour.

Paul, the 2nd oldest member of the group, decided to call it a day, because he wants to pursue other projects.

He's talking about setting up another band with a different musical direction completely (a rock band called SKUA). He's still going out with Hannah but he has admitted he will miss being together with her in S Club…

"I'll miss performing massively. That's what you do it for - the performing. You do it to get in front of a crowd and be an entertainer, because there's a part of you that loves the adoration of the crowd - that's why you do it."

He claims he was very worried about telling the group that he'd decided to leave, saying it was "terrifying… especially telling someone like Jon, because I'm quite close to him. Knowing how much he cares about the band, I didn't want to upset him."

Paul claims that Hannah knew that leaving the band was on his mind, but he soon made up his mind to do it, with no hard feelings about his experience with S Club 7 and no gripes about anyone else in the band.

Stories that Paul's new band is called Ralph's Trousers and their album is called Left-Handed Scooter Potato are completely false… that's just Paul being a little bit silly. Oh, how we'll miss his japes…

ACROSS

1. Where the 7 filmed their third TV series
5. She's the ex-dancer in the band
8. They're not boys.
9. It comes after the day!
10. Someone who pretends to be someone else for a living, ie on TV.
11. It's not the moon.
12. The realm of being a fan...
14. ——— Stop Moving
15. What kind of night you'd have with the band... (second song!)
19. What you become when you don't eat enough greens.
20. It's by the shore...
21. Tina's middle name.
22. What you need to dance and sing - food gives it to you.
25. What the Clubbers feel before a show.
26. ——— Of the Pops.
27. Get ——— and dance.

DOWN

1. She goes out with Paul
2. Not darken!
3. Go ____
4. What you do when you're shakin' you're thang.
5. What girls wear on their legs.
6. What melody is made up of.
7. The sun will do this in the morning.
13. If you stop doing something, don't stop doing this!
15. How many were there in the band in January 2002?
16. Someone who doesn't win...
17. What you wear as a jacket at school.
18. What's Jon's surname?
23. Crazy, or something you eat...
24. Recent S Club single...

Answers pages 62-63

BRADLEY
My Year

S CLUB

Has your year been...
a) Massive
b) Tiny
c) Cool
d) Hot!
e) Really rather exhausting actually
"It's been hot."

Have you taken up any new hobbies?
"I've got my laptop with me all the time now and my keyboard and I'm always writing songs."

What was your highlight of the year?
"It has to be all of it - winning an award for Don't Stop Movin' was heavy, the tour was good."

How do the band get on differently after three albums now? Do you still argue and if so, what about?
"Exactly the same, nothing's changed. We still argue, but we still have a great laugh."

How long is the longest it's ever taken a band member to wake you up Bradley?
"About an hour probably!"

Are there any rules you made on tour (ie the banning of smelly socks in the dressing room)?
"Just to have a great laugh but no we don't really have rules."

What was the most difficult thing about the tour?
a) the dancing
b) the singing
c) the lack of sleep
d) standing on the catwalk thinking it was going to fall down
e) not having enough Jaffa Cakes on the rider
f) not being able to have a kip mid-way through?
"No we always have a good sleep and I really got used to all of it, so none of it was really difficult."

What difference will Paul leaving make to the band?
"That there's only six of us."

If you could have anyone else living or dead to replace him, who would it be (Elvis, Elton John, Shirely Bassey)?
"I would say that he's irreplaceable but if I had to pick someone, it would be Cliff Richard, because the Jubilee gig with him went so well and he fitted in perfectly!"

If you could have done one thing differently this year, what would it have been?
"I would have kept my top on in the You video."

Any press stories which made you fume this year if yes, what were they?
"I don't really pay attention to them because they're mostly untrue and if they do write about me, it just amuses me."

Have you had any new nicknames this year?
"Wishbone and Leon (Spanish for Lion - my star sign)."

Lastly, what's been the best meal you've had this year and why was it so nice?
"I've only cooked once this year and my best meal was the one I cooked. It was jerk chicken and some rice and lasagne."

Oh, and second lastly, what's been the best item of clothing you've bought and why - does it make you look/feel truly amazing?
"I'm not really fussy on my clothes - I've worn a pair of combats for the first time this year and I really like them."

HANNAH
My Year

Has your year been...
a) Massive
b) Tiny
c) Cool
d) Hot!
e) Really rather exhausting actually
"All of them."

Have you taken up any new hobbies?
"Not really, I've got into cooking a little bit more. Everything used to be frozen food."

What was your highlight of the year?
"The Golden Jubilee."

How do the band get on differently after three albums now? Do you still argue and if so, what about?
"I think we get on better now. We don't really argue that much."

How long is the longest it's ever taken a band member to wake up Bradley?
"It's more of a case of spending half an hour then giving up."

Are there any rules you made on tour (ie the banning of smelly socks in the dressing room)
"There aren't really any rules."

What was the most difficult thing about the tour
a) the dancing
b) the singing
c) the lack of sleep
d) standing on the catwalk thinking it was going to fall down
e) not having enough Jaffa Cakes on the rider
f) not being able to have a kip mid-way through?
"The dance routines .... like Dance Dance Dance .... quite intense."

What difference will Paul leaving make to the band?
"We'll miss his humour, wackiness and general amusement."

If you could have anyone else living or dead to replace him, who would it be (Elvis, Elton John, Shirely Bassey)?
"Robbie Williams."

If you could have done one thing differently this year, what would it have been?
"I'd change nothing."

Any press stories which made you fume this year if yes, what were they?
"No, you never take them seriously and laugh them off."

Have you had any new nicknames this year?
"The same old nicknames stick - Spunjab, Hannah Banana."

Lastly, what's been the best meal you've had this year and why was it so nice?
"Japanese - out here in Barcelona."

Oh, and second lastly, what's been the best item of clothing you've bought and why - does it make you look/feel truly amazing?
"I haven't really bought much this year - one of my favourite tops is a little red top my sister made me."

JO
My Year

Has your year been...
a) Massive
b) Tiny
c) Cool
d) Hot!
e) Really rather exhausting actually
"Very exhausting!"

Have you taken up any new hobbies?
"Horse riding."

What was your highlight of the year?
"The Jubilee and the tour - it's a close call between them."

How do the band get on differently after three albums now? Do you still argue and if so, what about?
"We argue less now cos we all understand each other more, we just laugh at things more."

How long is the longest it's ever taken a band member to wake up Bradley?
"Hours sometimes."

Are there any rules you made on tour (ie the banning of smelly socks in the dressing room)
"No, not really."

What was the most difficult thing about the tour
a) the dancing
b) the singing
c) the lack of sleep
d) standing on the catwalk thinking it was going to fall down
e) not having enough Jaffa Cakes on the rider
f) not being able to have a kip mid-way through?
"Singing live and dancing at the same time."

What difference will Paul leaving make to the band?
"His spur of the moment funniness."

If you could have anyone else living or dead to replace him, who would it be (Elvis, Elton John, Shirely Bassey)?
"Paul's irreplaceable! (Or if pushed Brad Pitt...)"

If you could have done one thing differently this year, what would it have been?
"I wouldn't have eaten so much chocolate."

Any press stories which made you fume this year if yes, what were they?
"None as yet."

Have you had any new nicknames this year?
"Roller Girl."

Lastly, what's been the best meal you've had this year and why was it so nice?
"Probably here in Barcelona in the Hotel Arts - lobster and sea bass."

Oh, and second lastly, what's been the best item of clothing you've bought and why - does it make you look/feel truly amazing?
"I haven't really bought anything outstanding this year."

Has your year been...
a) Massive
b) Tiny
c) Cool
d) Hot!
e) Really rather exhausting actually
"Really rather exhausting actually!"

Describe the way you have individually blossomed as a person?
"I think I've definitely become a lot more confident within myself and a lot happier. In particular this year we did a lot of major things - we got a lot of credit this year and it felt good to be in S Club."

Have you taken up any new hobbies?
"Just before last June I got my horse - I've been riding a lot and that pretty much takes up all my time when I'm not working."

What was your highlight of the year?
"The tour is always good - that is always a pinnacle for us as it really does hit home how successful we've become. But the Jubilee does have to be the peak as it was such a historical event and it was great to be a part of it."

How do the band get on differently after three albums now? Do you still argue and if so, what about?
"We've never really majorly argued. We still have our little niggles but at this particular moment in time, we're closer than we've ever been."

How long is the longest it's ever taken a band member to wake up Bradley?
"There was one time he was three hours late for a TV recording."

Are there any rules you made on tour (ie the banning of smelly socks in the dressing room)
"Just to have as much fun as possible and go out every night."

What was the most difficult thing about the tour
a) the dancing
b) the singing
c) the lack of sleep
d) standing on the catwalk thinking it was going to fall down
e) not having enough Jaffa Cakes on the rider
f) not being able to have a kip mid-way through?
"I'd say not having enough sleep as we were promoting You at the same time so that made it a lot harder - getting up at 6am in the morning instead of 2pm."

What difference will Paul leaving make to the band?
"I think its made everyone focus a lot more on what they want to do. I think it's going to make us better, no disrespect. History has proven that if a band member leaves, the band normally splits up but we don't want that to happen so we're really gonna go for it and be the best we can be."

If you could have anyone else living or dead to replace him, who would it be (Elvis, Elton John, Shirely Bassey)?
"Elvis Presley."

Do you think Paul will want to come back to the group 'cos he'll get jealous?
"No, Paul left 'cos he'd had enough. He's really happy and it was so nice to finish on a good note. It doesn't actually feel like he's left as he's still popping in and we're all really good friends with him."

What were your personal highlights during the year?
"I think my 20th birthday was a highlight no longer being a teenager, definitely a big step. And I think the tour was a really big thing for me."

If you could have done one thing differently this year, what would it have been?
"I can't think of anything specific but there are always times throughout the whole experience when you look back and see it was such a wicked thing, that I wish I'd had more fun with it at the time and appreciated it at the time."

Any press stories which made you fume this year if yes, what were they?
"All the stuff about Hannah leaving the band was annoying because it is total rubbish, but mostly I take no notice."

Have you had any new nicknames this year?
"Ivan (it means Jon in Russian)."

Lastly, what's been the best meal you've had this year and why was it so nice?
"All the Spanish food is lovely here in Spain as we film the new TV series, but I don't have a favourite meal as such."

Oh, and second lastly, what's been the best item of clothing you've bought and why - does it make you look/feel truly amazing?
"I got a really nice suit - black suit with red pinstripes - it's wicked."

RACHEL
My Year

S CLUB

Has your year been...
a) Massive
b) Tiny
c) Cool
d) Hot!
e) Really rather exhausting actually
"Massive and hot, very hot and cool and tiring."

Have you taken up any new hobbies?
"No, nothing new this year"

What was your highlight of the year
"The Golden Jubilee where we played at Buckingham Palace, and the Carnival tour, The Brits and Record of the Year."

How do the band get on differently after three albums now? Do you still argue and if so, what about?
"We argue but not really that much. I don't think we get on differently, if anything we kind of understand each other more."

How long is the longest it's ever taken a band member to wake up Bradley?
"I don't know, it's always management who wake him - I don't know if I've ever tried to wake him up."

Are there any rules you made on tour (ie the banning of smelly socks in the dressing room)
"None really."

What was the most difficult thing about the tour
a) the dancing
b) the singing
c) the lack of sleep
d) standing on the catwalk thinking it was going to fall down
e) not having enough Jaffa Cakes on the rider
f) not being able to have a kip mid-way through?
"The quick changes were always a bit mad.

What difference will Paul leaving make to the band?
"We will miss his mad dance moves he comes out with and having that older guy around and a mate."

If you could have anyone else living or dead to replace him, who would it be (Elvis, Elton John, Shirely Bassey)?
"Robbie Williams."

Do you think Paul will want to come back to the group 'cos he'll get jealous?
"No, I think it will be funny for him sometimes, but I don't think he'd ever want to come back. He's happy doing his own thing but I'm sure we will keep in touch with him!"

If you could have done one thing differently this year, what would it have been?
"I'd probably not change anything. I think you learn from your mistakes and it can make you a stronger person."

Any press stories which made you fume this year if yes, what were they?
"No, not really."

Have you had any new nicknames this year?
"Princess is my new nickname."

Lastly, what's been the best meal you've had this year and why was it so nice?
"I always look forward to having a really nice roast dinner at my local pub whenever we've been away or a good Chinese or Indian."

Oh, and second lastly, what's been the best item of clothing you've bought and why - does it make you look/feel truly amazing?
"I've bought lots this year, but I haven't really got a favourite item of clothing."

TINA
My Year

Has your year been...
a) Massive
b) Tiny
c) Cool
d) Hot!
e) Really rather exhausting actually
"A mixture of all of them I guess."

Have you taken up any new hobbies?
"I've started songwriting a lot more - I've always written poetry."

What was your highlight of the year?
"Everything played a big part but nothing beats singing live on tour to the fans."

How do the band get on differently after three albums now? Do you still argue and if so, what about?
"We still get on - there are arguments but nothing major."

How long is the longest it's ever taken a band member to wake up Bradley?
"I've never really tried to wake him, but I think it's funny actually."

Are there any rules you made on tour (ie the banning of smelly socks in the dressing room)
"No."

What was the most difficult thing about the tour
a) the dancing
b) the singing
c) the lack of sleep
d) standing on the catwalk thinking it was going to fall down
e) not having enough Jaffa Cakes on the rider
f) not being able to have a kip mid-way through?
"I guess the singing was the most difficult because if you're voice doesn't feel right, it doesn't sound right and nerves play a part - if you're nervous, you can hear it when you sing."

What difference will Paul leaving make to the band?
"We won't have his character or his energy, but on the positive side photoshoots will be a lot easier. Ha ha"

If you could have anyone else living or dead to replace him, who would it be (Elvis, Elton John, Shirely Bassey)?
"Someone like Jamie Oliver, the Naked Chef, then we'd eat good food."

What were your personal highlights during the year?
"Finding more out about the business and feeling more at home with it as weird as it can be."

If you could have done one thing differently this year, what would it have been?
"I would have had more time to myself."

Any press stories which made you fume this year if yes, what were they?
"I take the press stories with a pinch of salt."

Have you had any new nicknames this year?
"Queenie and Tina Marie."

Lastly, what's been the best meal you've had this year and why was it so nice?
"When I went to Bibendum in London - the food's great."

Oh, and second lastly, what's been the best item of clothing you've bought and why - does it make you look/feel truly amazing?
"The jeans our stylist, Kenny Ho, bought me - I've never been a fan of hipster jeans, but these have converted me. I never thought I'd feel that decent in a pair of hipsters!"

Wordsearch 2

More words below for you to find in the grid mix?

```
B N L K S E D G N I X I M
F A L S E N O H P D A E H
M M C T E Y C D R O L B C
I R O K L I T H R L B E A
C N G U I T A R O U U A O
R O M E V N T L S R M T C
O S H H E B G O S O U S G
P C T G R O O V E U U S N
H A Y M O R O R O C K L I
O L H T O O B L A C O V G
N E R V M T U N E R A O N
E V E R S E K B A S S L I
P O P L K E Y B O A R D S
```

Rock
Tune
Vocal booth
Singing coach
Scale
Mixing desk
Guitar
Drums
Bass
Keyboards
Pop
Microphone
Key
Headphones
Backing vocals
Rhythm
Groove
Album
Beats
Soul
Live room
Chorus
Verse
Note

Answers pages 62-63

MASH LYRICS

Here are some lyrics from the previous S Club 7 Albums, and we've replaced one word with 'mash' and one with 'sausage' - which word does it replace?

1. Best mash, never gonna let you down
   Best mash, always gonna be around
   You know whatever sausage puts you through
   I'll be there for you
   We all need a best mash to understand
   A best mash to take your hand
   You know whatever sausage puts you through
   I'll be there for you

2. We'll spend the whole time grooving
   Cos what we really like is to sausage on Friday night
   I got my friends and we're here to groove (na na na na na na)
   Nothing's wrong, ain't nothin' to prove (na na na na na na)
   Don't need no mash just bring a friend (na na na na na na)
   Cos we're gonna sausage all night again (na na na na na na)
   One can make a sausage
   Two is not enough to get down
   Three you'll still get lonely cos tonight's the night for crowds

3. It's been a long sausage, girl, but I'll keep on waiting
   I'll keep waiting till that day when
   You come home, come home to me
   Life's too short to live without you
   Where you are is where I wanna be
   Hey mash, it's a matter of sausage
   Before you come on home and I get what's mine

4. Mash, mash, mash
   Come on and do it baby
   Mash, mash, mash
   Sausage it up, sausage it out
   Mash, mash, mash
   Just keep it movin' on the mash floor boogie
   on the mash floor boogie woogie
   It's everywhere, it's in everything
   We're getting down and the whole place is moving

5. I'm the right mash
   Ooh, I'm the right mash for you
   If all you need's good sausage
   Look no further, come to me
   I'm the right mash
   Ooh, I'm the right mash for you

Answers pages 62-63

DESIGN A
T-SHIRT
AND WIN!

Take part in our exciting competition and you can win!

All you have to do, using the outline below, is design a t-shirt for one of the band onto the paper, describing any special fabrics or accessories you've used. The best few will be shown on the S Club web site (www.sclub.com) and the winner will get 4 tickets to their nearest S Club gig in April. Send your completed entries to arrive not later than 28 February 2003 to:

S CLUB DESIGN A T-SHIRT COMPETITION
Pedigree Books
The Old Rectory
Matford Lane
Exeter
EX2 4PS

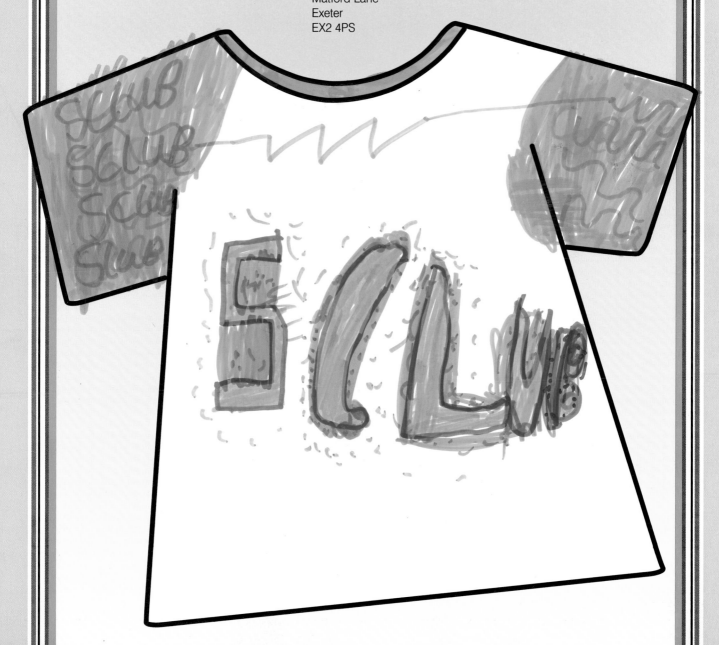

WHAT'S COMING UP

S Club were in Spain (where they answered their My Year questions - hence the references to Barcelona), working very hard on their new series.

One thing that they're still trying to get used to is the fact that Paul isn't around. The band admit that they are finding it strange but are learning to deal with it.

"It does feel strange," says Bradley. "Especially when we're working on dance routines for just six people! We're getting used to it though and Paul's just popped over to see Hannah, which is wicked. It's really cool for all of us to catch up with him."

But then he had to go! Still, the S Clubbers have plenty to do when they're not on camera. They've been hiring videos, going to the gym and trying out the local restaurants - see their My Year answers - so it seems they're getting a taste for Spanish food…

Jo and Rachel spent the afternoon sightseeing; sitting on top of a tour bus in Barcelona town - and managed not to get recognised once! Tina's been sunbathing and managing to burn her face while Bradley's found a local nightclub whose tunes he really rates - which means it's harder than ever to get the band's resident sleepy head out of bed…

The S Clubbers are also planning an S Club movie, to be filmed in Autumn 2002. The project is still being finalised at the moment, so there's little detail, but it's definitely an adventure with their music of course and it's sure to show off the S Club vibe and be full of wild adventures - a *big* version of the S Club series.

Then there's the S Club tour, with the S Club Juniors, which will be rockin' the houses in April. The dates so far are as follows…

- Wednesday 2nd April - Glasgow SECC
- Thursday 3rd April - Glasgow SECC
- Saturday 5th April - Newcastle Telewest Arena
- Tuesday 8th April - Sheffield Arena
- Wednesday 9th April - Sheffield Arena
- Saturday 12th April - Manchester Evening News Arena
- Tuesday 15th April - Birmingham NEC
- Wednesday 16th April - Birmingham NEC
- Saturday 19th April - London Docklands Arena
- Sunday 20th April - London Docklands Arena
- Wednesday 23rd April - Wembley Arena
- Thursday 24th April - Wembley Arena

S CLUB ACTIVITY

PAGE 11
WORDSEARCH 1

PAGES 12+13
S CLUB 7 SWOT

1. Jo
2. Clint
3. Bradley
4. Will, Gareth and Darius
5. Paul and Hannah
6. Jo
7. Superman
8. Rachel
9. Tina
10. Tina
11. Hannah
12. Bradley
13. A remote control car
14. Paul

CAR Trouble?

Who owns which car?
a) Rachel
b) Hannah
c) Tina
d) Paul

PAGE 22
IN THE MIX

1. Video
2. Outfits
3. Routine
4. TV Show
5. Tour
6. New Song

PAGES 23+24
S CLUB 7 IN QUOTES

a) Bradley
b) Jo
c) Paul
d) Rachel
e) Hannah
f) Jon
g) Bradley
h) Jon
i) Bradley
j) Paul
k) Rachel
l) Hannah
m) Tina
n) Bradley
o) Paul

PAGE 33
WHERE AM I?

TINA: Liverpool
JON: Birmingham
HANNAH: Brighton
PAUL: London
BRADLEY: Cardiff
RACHEL: Edinburgh
JO: Dublin

PAGE 45
TRUE OR FALSE

1. False, 2. False, 3. True,
4. True, 5. True, 6. False,
7. False

NAME GAME

ANSWER: Wembley Arena

PAGE 48
CROSSWORD

PAGE 55
WORDSEARCH 2

S **62** CLUB